POETRY BIRMINGHAM

POETRY BIRMINGHAM
Literary Journal

Spring 2020 — Issue Three

EDITOR

Suna Afshan

PALLINA PRESS LIMITED.
BIRMINGHAM

POETRY BIRMINGHAM
Literary Journal

Pallina Press Limited, Birmingham
www.pallinapress.com

Typeset & Design: Suna Afshan, Adrian B. Earle, and Naush Sabah
Co-editor: Naush Sabah

ISSN 2633-0822
ISBN 9798615426674

COVER IMAGE

Dead Game, 1829
By Edward Coleman
Photo by Birmingham Museums Trust, licensed under Creative Commons CC0

Birmingham
Museums

SUBMISSIONS

For our guidelines, visit www.poetrybirmingham.com

Submission windows:
1st to 31st March
1st to 30th June
1st to 31st October

'Hope' is the thing with feathers –
That perches in the soul –
And sings the tune without the words –
And never stops – at all –

'314', Emily Dickinson

More safe I Sing with mortal voice, unchang'd
To hoarce or mute, though fall'n on evil dayes,
On evil dayes though fall'n, and evil tongues;
In darkness, and with dangers compast round,
And solitude; yet not alone, while thou
Visit'st my slumbers Nightly, or when Morn
Purples the East: still govern thou my Song,
Urania, and fit audience find, though few.

'Paradise Lost', John Milton

Go, go, go, said the bird: human kind
Cannot bear very much reality.
Time past and time future
What might have been and what has been
Point to one end, which is always present.

'Burnt Norton', T. S. Eliot

CONTENTS

EDITORIAL

Suna Afshan

The Pursuit of the Real

I drink one ristretto at the counter, and I take another to the table to savour. It's a Wednesday, so I edit. A man approaches—white, elderly, innocuous— he takes the seat beside me. Two minutes pass and I'm certain he's scalded his tongue on his tea, given how quickly he sets the mug down, how during the conversation which unfolds, he scrapes his frilly tongue against his teeth, winces. His children—three, middle-aged—live in the Wirral, his wife is dead. He worked as a ticket-collector on Manchester buses, and later on the trains. I tell him about *this* job.

'I'm sorry,' he says, 'you'll have to explain. What does a poetry editor do?'

•

. . . every day one can see signs indicating that now, at the present moment, something new, and on a scale never witnessed before, is being born: humanity as an elemental force conscious of transcending Nature, for it lives by memory of itself, that is, in History.

In 1982, under Harvard's Charles Eliot Norton Professorship of Poetry, Czeslaw Milosz concluded a lecture entitled 'On Hope' with the above words.

15

The lecture now serves many darkly ironic moments, so much so that my copy of *The Witness of Poetry*—the book of all his published lectures as professor—is littered with exclamation marks in the margins, an occasional 'lol'. 'A decline of civic virtues is occurring in the West,' he says, and later, 'as the century draws to its close, there is no doubt left as to the parasitic character of any state based upon a monopoly of ownership and power'. Indeed, and the parasite has undeniably latched itself to the host, taken over. But the lecture itself, I find, is riddled with a parasite more cunning and more sly than the State: hope. 'Humanity will increasingly be turning back to itself,' says Milosz, 'increasingly contemplating its entire past, searching for a key to its own enigma, and penetrating, through empathy, the soul of bygone generations and of whole civilisations'. And I see that in the poems in this issue of *Poetry Birmingham*— the interrogation of lost voices, of time, of that ether in which the marble floats 'throttled, violated'—but beyond poetry? Beyond art itself? Is humanity needling with *empathy* through the past, or mining it for its most repugnant ideas?

This century is one of truth debased: we are in Nero's Rome, the mint has taken a potato peeler to the silver coinage. Blinkered philosophies are the pith of current political discourse, the language of which is 'shallow and threadbare', says Armitage, not 'feeling like it has any truthfulness at all'; and if in 1982 Milosz said, 'the media are for the mind what too-small slippers were for women's feet in old China', I imagine it would be rather close to scaphism now . . . 'There was a moral.' Nevertheless, for those factions of society, which believe 'what we never knew and what we didn't see / didn't happen', history is not something that must be interrogated for bias or illusions, debated, penetrated with empathy, for it is a mere fiction. Fact, too, is a debased currency. I had an unfortunate stint as a soft-solipsist when I was seventeen, after taking a single philosophy module at college: the felled trees were soundless, 'no relentless onomatopoeia / of footfall and a shush / hissed across buildings', no need for those chatrooms 'for the Amish and the Hutterites'. How does one reconcile this insular right-wing populism with all of its ironies?

Heaney wrote in *The Door Stands Open* that Milosz called upon poetry to 'combat death and nothingness'. *True* poetry was, to Milosz, 'the passionate pursuit of the Real'. Poets in the throes of this pursuit, commit decades of their life to the keeping of morning papers—that ablution of the mind—, shun their loved ones and retire to PVC conservatories, spend hours watching the magpie couple pick at the fluorescent moss in the gutter, and perhaps come to the conclusion that these words they've jotted down are as close to anything real they've experienced. Though, it must be stated, 'real' and 'truth' are not interchangeable in the poem's domain. A poem is a papier-mâchéd urn of truths, held together by the tricks of lyric and form; if left to stand under its own weight, the poem shall only *just* be porcelain-strong, but it will be real, nonetheless. In those experiences of exorcizing the poem, where it seems to warrants something *more*, and 'nothing less than the unification of [psychological] personality', as put by Breton, will suffice, poetry's relationship with truth becomes one of coaxing, cooing, and the creature which emerges from all the usual hiding places, a changeling: 'a soggy paper fairy child', fearing 'the cut of iron scissors // And judicious editors'.

Before founding this journal, the great poet-editor relationships, for me, occupied the same space as parable: Wordsworth and Coleridge; Tennyson and Hallam; Eliot and Pound. If *true* poetry sincerely is 'the passionate pursuit of the real', I wonder how much the western 'canon' owes to its poetry editors for their work in reifying the real. Because the editorial act requires nothing less than the metamorphosis of the Self; it is not a disengaged and disembodied perusal of the poem: no, we, for a time, rent a room in the poet's home, map its dimensions, we check the relative tidiness of cutlery drawers, and figure out the way the shower operates. And only equipped with this familiarity, may we venture out, perhaps 'dig over the roses' with 'some bright idea / of what a garden should look like', foist cold spectres of ideas 'out of the upset under-places'. These conversations between the poet and the editor form an intellectual and spiritual exchange, that as a poet I've found indispensable, and as an editor, sacrosanct. Line-editing, specifically, deserves recognition as *the* essential part of the editor-poet relationship, and therefore must be preserved practice in the publication cycle of literary periodicals. However, in the discussions which have taken place with poets this past year, and particularly in this issue of *Poetry Birmingham*, it has become apparent that a dwindling of editorial responsibility—nothing less than a debasement—is occurring.

This is a literary culture too contingent on nebulous avowals of acclaim or censure, so I believe there's a renewed need for editorial attention based on the specifics of poems. Yes, this is a century not only of debased truth, but it is also defined on its willingness to procrastinate over course-correction: we see that clearly in political doublespeak—'a language under the language'—and in the continued decimation of the natural climate. Milosz's brand of hope entered the rubric of reality because he foresaw humanity with its jaws forever locked around the tail of entropy. In the face of this, it seems that I too, like Milosz, am host to that parasite, resolved to hope. Because 'when the floods clear what will be left, washed up / at our gate or lodges between the polite // paving stones along our tree-lines road?'; what will be left of poetry?

John Greening

Augural Address

The big man in the spotlight of reality steps over
to open the last executive box. Out fly the ravens,

making a clapping sound, uttering the only words
they've learnt from the dark, never more to be guards

with clipped wings outside a foreign tower, nor perched
on shoulders of a foreign god. These birds have watched

the centuries since their very first mission, to locate
a new world for entrepeneurs. In the dying light

he follows them, and nods as they head towards Russia,
smiling as they pass across the steppes of Central Asia,

then lock on to their targets, repeating *Great, Great.*
Those who are hoping for the dove to appear will have to wait.

GREGORY LEADBETTER

Lord of Misrule
for Ian Marchant

Throwing up at the result of that referendum
My hot graffiti dripping from Parliament
   I bequeath thee shitte
Spamming every feed and trending now
The remedy, I say to the tired Christ
Slack in my skin
Is to be drunk, 'on wine, poetry or virtue, as you wish'
Preferably all three at once.
O for some Weimar easy virtue, given wisely
To snuff the insolence of office out
And dance a tango
Through their sober death.
I mean to teach these suits morality.

After a dunk in the Thames, black as oil,
I board my zeppelin.
Far below, the city streets are floes of fire.
Pepys runs to bury his wheel of Parmesan cheese.
He, at least, takes my advice.

You are invited to the Feast of Fools.
Come dressed as the century,
Each of you a prophecy.
I will supply a little theatre.

Pale mummers, their tongues all told,
Haunt year zero:
Remind you that the dead can live
And will perform for food.
Will Kempe in his cap and bells
Dances a morris to Primal Scream
And conjures a crocus from broken earth.
The homeless, housed in Kensington
Drop pennies into the cups of royal rough sleepers
Cold on their thrones.
Those who once made money out of money
Even in 'crisis'
Find life in laying a hedge of hazel and willow
In the Midlands style.
I thought er wuz jed, one says, audible

Tears in the voice he has found in his blood.
I thought er wuz jed, an the spudgucks n'all
But they ay, they ay
Er's in this wand, an the spudgucks n'all.

Our revels last three days of night.
The players breed with the crowd.
When at last the lights go out
I let a full breast slip from my dress,
Dance with the living and the dead
Our mouths at our necks
Until Albion shudders its *petite mort.*

The suits drop their jaws, enlightened.

Shh. Go easy on that hungover head.
There are those who would hang us by an ankle
Until we bleed dry.
I play myself as a Tarot card
To see their fear eye to eye.

They will trespass at dawn
To drag me from my enseamèd bed
In the name of the crime they've dressed as the law
And ungratefully frame my jest as offence.
Someone will shout: My poor fool is hanged
But I will wink
From the gallows
When they think
I am dead.

DANIEL HINDS

Nine Spilt Yolks

From the speckled hen nine eggs I stole,
The Fairy Changeling, Dora Sigerson Shorter

I

Something I'll never know
Was stolen right out from under my tongue.

And in its place I unfurled
A soggy paper fairy child.

Some scrap of fallen faerie wisdom
That babbles like a baby, pretending to be a man,
Or a brook, pretending to be a steaming pot,
Growing hot upon the hearth.

II

Paper child,

Your infant call keeps me awake all night.
I swaddle you in white robes, share in the second sight
Of your apposition eyes. Sometimes, I ignore your bawling,
Roll over, rest and regret the blank page come morning,

When I can no longer see by day's decaying light
Whatever strange and sickle shape you held.

Other times, the gift is just a goblin
Gobbledegook trick. You laugh and leave me
A hex: untranslatable fayerye talk
Hoaxed on browning leaves,

Curling, like a monument to burnt parchment.

III

Sometimes, I scrub the muck off of you
And you disintegrate
In the bathtub

As if I'd boiled you with the eggshells.

When the dirty tub water transforms into a Naiad's laughter,
It's easy to throw the baby out with the bathwater.

IV

You're lucky you weren't born in a grimmer wooded age,
When witches and woodcutters wandered
The swallowed, beaten, breadcrumb path;
When some rustic rhymer would have gathered
Logs, and courage, and poverty's hungry unnamed
Necessity—and thrown you into the flames.

Now, more likely,
A wastepaper basket—
Squash you up squirming
And still shrill jabbering
With my other aborted litter.

Next day, lift you out,
Uncrease your little wrinkled body,
Hold you up to my loving breast

And interrogating eyes.

V

Infant migrant of Tuatha Dé Danann,
The girlish boyish wailing go-between,
The child of two worlds.

VI

Sum of all my days, I waste before
Your unending appetite for my life,
My thoughts, my loves, my dreams.

Sometimes I wear the seams inside
Out so you can't get to me
With your suckling screams.

Your pudgy pixie hands have an iron grip,
But I know you fear the cut of iron scissors

And judicious editors.

VII

Faerie.
Even the word does not stay still.

Fairye, let me hear

The fluid and formal first words that every mother dreads,
But every poet longs to hear, the child's laugh and ancient cheer,
For novelty new born upon the earth, brewed and boiled
In the grail of an eggshell cup:

'I am as ancient as all the woods of the west,
And all the painted paper in which I am dressed,
But never have I seen or been such a thing before,
Though my lean tongue is tired and my hard heels sore.'

Your feet tread on eggshells; their crack is your speech.

VIII

Sometimes, I hear

Far away, and half forgotten,
The music of a humdrum child kept
Beneath a pillared and rising hill.

On the shadowed side of some fayre Sidhe,
A tithe to hell traded for a leaf of laurel lay

Teethes in an inferno's maw.

I know we're not supposed to have favourites, but
I love you more than any weak, wan, womb-born whelp.

IX

Changeling child,

You wear thin; you wear thin pale eggshell skin,
A hefty egg-shaped head, and speckled spriggan skin.

I clothe you in my own flesh;
A babygrow for a baby that will never grow.

I have a father's torn beard, and a mother's suckled breast,
And the papers hate a single parent best.

When I've tossed you into the fires
A little yellow head surfaces, burbles, pops up

From a sizzling egg yolk.

Before Thunder

In dank waters
hands float like lilies.
And the Tigris,
that bore civilization
like mother earth
on uneven shoulders,
runs, a brown wound,
between factions.

Wasps swarm
above my lover's window.
They have made their home
above our bed.
Next year they will swarm
in some other place.
Above your grave, I wonder.

Such fertility in me—
my mind bleeds words.
In the bushes beyond gardens
a vixen screams in the dark,
engendering the night.

There's no answer to it.
I want wit less than justice
and wit enough to bear it;
a sudden lightning flash
breaking into the music
like a stutter.

The sky is dark tonight.
The sky is full of dust
and thunderflies.
The light is reflected
like a giant moon
curved as a woman's belly.
Man is always deceived
by mirrors that pretend
to be windows.

My keys lie next
to glass and comb.
I could take them up
and drive down
the night-time fox
and moths like ticker tape.
I could drive myself down,
draw the sheets of lightning
over my head
and close my eyes.

Women bear their destruction
within them like rotten fruit.
There is a sweetness there
that exceeds taste.
Only the snake can get
his tongue about our seed.
And there is a bitterness
that exceeds gall.
The wasp eats all
and then moves on.

It has become hard for me
to speak of it.
Your blood beat overtakes mine
and then suddenly I wait,
as an audience at the final note,
as children delighted and scared
before thunder.
We demand continuity
and we are denied
by blood and by music.
We fill finality
with applause.

James O'Hara-Knight

Impressions of Missing Matter

>] for
>] lightly
>] reminded me now of Anaktoria
> who is gone.
>
> Sappho, 'Fragment 16', trans. Anne Carson

She slipped me out to benches
and we assimilated gin under the awning;
asked that I divulge
who had touched me so crucially
that I could no longer take shuttle in hand?
And I might have fallen back—

her eyes were too big, too lucid,
spun in parataxis:
a boy, her lust, spirit clutched.
Swiftly we affirmed, *desiderium sinus cordis*.

We thought the more we stood out of the way
the more Sappho showed through.

That which is here is not here.
Glass capitulates. Space opens onto space.
Carson's brackets capture Sappho's missing matter.

We pointed lit fags like manicules
to those absences we had closest at hand,
long gaps in the traffic on Farringdon Road.
The N63 turns its lambent nose
attempting new ways to say,
Hector is dead and a shiver sweeps Troy.

She said it was a professor's love
which had rent her most deeply
and that tonight, like a square bracket,
the remembered affair implied a free space—
Clerkenwell, King's Cross, Holborn—
not an accurate record but a gesture towards
the papyrological event,

that in translation we might not miss
the drama of trying to read the sleeping figure:
someone else's papyrus body in the morning,
torn in half or riddled with holes.

Ruth Aylett

Iseult's Complaint

You won't need that surge of violins
where we're going, if you can follow me,
musician, into the nuked badlands.

Tristan died old, his looks lost twenty years ago,
there was no room in the cardboard coffin
for the crematorium to immolate me.

I left a rose on top as the curtains closed
and turned away. Only wild and beautiful lovers
make headlines, so go on, perform your myth again.

Love and death, death and love. What's the music
for habit and comfort, shopping together,
arms round shoulders, the times I cut his hair?

EMILY PRITCHARD

The Night Kitchen

After we speak tonight
I make brownies.
The kind of evening baking
where the day recedes
and a calm purpose opens
up the night.
           I love a recipe:
the numbered steps, the adjectives,
the second person. I whisk
eggs and sugar until the mix
is *thick and creamy as milkshake*,
melt butter with broken
squares of chocolate
until smooth, then fold
the two together.
           The trick,
the recipe says, *to marry them
without knocking out the air, so be as slow
and gentle as you like.* Slow as I go, gentle
as I try to be, my arm aches more
than beating batter makes it.
           To fold
takes patience, to weave
dark into light like waiting
for a pattern to emerge
from coloured threads.
*Stop just before you think
              you should.*
And this is butch; to lift
the heavy bowl and pour
the mix into the tray.
I don't know how to fix things
but tonight, my white shirt
stained with chocolate,
I make something good
to give to you.

HILAIRE

For Perfect Pastry

O to be born with bloodless hands,
pre-chilled fingers
to rub butter into flour
into breadcrumb texture.

Work in a cool kitchen:
shuttered windows, stone floor,
a breath of *Gironde* air
through the doorstopped door.

Observe the rituals
before you begin. Roll out
your shoulders. Dampen butterflies
with a nip of Cognac or gin.

Your best friend is a marble
rolling pin. Test her weight,
her clout, in the palm of your hand.
Let no one enter your domain.

L. KIEW

Laundry

Discarded days ago, your shirt
sleeves droop despondently over
the plastic rim onto the floor,
cuffs trailing the dust.
Like a brown cat, my skirt rubs
static against black trousers,
knickers and a solitary red sock,
a hole in the heart of its heel.

Emptying the basket, I face
our stained Lycra, a heptagon,
its reverse commemorating
the fiftieth anniversary of the NHS,
a crust of tissues, a parking ticket
and a button from that dress,
the blue one I was wearing
when you kissed the ventilator.

Richie McCaffery

Exercise Bike

The best gift Mam's got Dad
is the exercise bike. He's on it
every day, cycling the distance
of the village to the city and back.

In a week he's done hundreds
of miles still tethered
to the backroom. Mam says
he's growing fearful driving

to work and he hates it when
he gets there. He keeps
himself fit by getting nowhere.
When Grandma broke her hip

and would have no one care
for her but Dad, he took
the bike to hers, adding
hours to his daily commute.

He couldn't eat in her presence
because of childhood trauma,
so he starved and dreamed
of peddling to Burger King

late at night, and wolfing
down convenience food
in the midst of the most
inconvenient life.

Lynn Harding

Acting

Magnets on the fridge
spell new words
seven sheep orange truck
a language fluent in innocence
you have forgotten.
A superhero lunch box
hangs from a hook on the wall.
You warn me of things that are not frightening
a small boy upstairs we must not wake
the lack of fresh milk
impending morning
as though to distract me
from fingers
seeking crevices, pulling my hair
and your left leg
shivering

I try to understand
what message you read.
Was I too coy
with my cup of tea?
Did I gasp
as its liquid heat
met my lips
trace my tongue
along the rim?

Pasta dries in the sink
I make my excuses.

You sleep alone
no sheep to count
no number on a napkin.

MARK RUSSELL

Director of Photography

Our garden backs on to the school yard
with a view of the cricket ground beyond.

I slice and fry garlic and peppers,
open tins of tuna and sweetcorn.

I can hear my son and his friends woop
playing football, and see my daughter

ignore them as she swings back and forth,
delighting in the absence of pressure.

I wonder how I might capture this
on a reel of film, store it in my basement

and one day ask my carer
to go down and find the one

marked: *it was the summer*
of nothing but space and time

and we can sit around and watch
the movement of one within the other.

Forty-Forty-In

Kevin's too quick for me. In a sprint from the kiosk to the water fountain, I lose every time plus one. When he shuts his eyes, I climb the tree that overhangs him, straddle a branch, listen as he counts to forty, watch him slide off into the park, long black hair, tight blue jeans, past the oak we use for cricket, where he once clean bowled an actual Australian with his fast swinging wrong-foot delivery. When he turns to see me hanging, waiting for him, I know he is judging whether he can run faster than I can let go, fall, gather myself, and reach out to touch the tall silver basin. To beat him. He is deciding if he should put his faith in brutality, wondering if I'll ever know he has no choice.

LUKE KENNARD

Three Poems *from* 'Notes on the Sonnets'

6

I had a dream that there were ten of you and we lived in a duplex overlooking
the river. It was the only nice part of town. I wanted to make ten of you happy,
but it was difficult and mostly I felt like I was letting at least eight of you down.
Even though the ten of you were exactly you and exactly the same, you cannot
stroke ten people's hair and tell them they are good, they are so good, and oh
the divergent seconds where lived experience changed you. Even the inanities,
I love what you've done to your hair. Is that a new top? Could you just shift over
a little? I didn't think I was up to the job. So, this is a job for you? I don't want
to make any special claims here: nobody ever walked down to a river without
at least considering taking a dive. We only owned nine mugs, for instance, and
it only struck me years later, snow-fishing in a void I'd learned to wrap around
myself, how easy it would have been for me to do something about that.

36

Did they confuse our orders? We met because they confused our orders. It was a restaurant. Or we were in the army. Either way it was inevitable that we would meet exchanging plates or inscrutable codes over the border. We met because we joined the same cult and escaped together just before the shooting started. It was a cult we co-founded, but so conveniently wrong for us. We met because you still have the dream-catchers. I wish you'd take them down, not because they embarrass me, but because they've caught too many dreams and you're not even using them. We met when the cult begged us to rejoin because it wasn't the same without us.

Sometimes nostalgia is just a self-microwaving cup of coffee which will never cool sufficiently to bring it to your lips. A build-up to the first kiss like a ski-lift; on a ski-lift. As a child I felt it necessary to apologise for being a child. As an adult not so much. Sometimes it is necessary to retrace your steps just in case you find yourself lying by the side of the river. It's fun until it isn't. Sometimes nostalgia can be likened to a man who owns a vineyard. He goes down to the marketplace to find workers to gather the grapes, but instead . . . how does it go? They kill him and his son and set fire to the vineyard. There was a moral. We met because there was a moral.

120

The first computer-generated apology was so graceful and convincing people assumed it was fake, that there was someone inside the casing operating tiny levers, but there wasn't. It created all sorts of possibilities. Soon it was accepted that most relationships could benefit from some degree of artificial optimisation via basic logic gates. We really listened to each other. When you do that, this is how it makes me feel. I'm not saying it's reasonable, but it's the reason I react the way I do. I'm sorry I made you feel like that. God, I love the long shadows in the evening. I'll try to be more aware of my tendency to . . . No, it's okay—I know I'm oversensitive and you're so kind to me. I know you didn't want or mean to make me feel like that. Yeah, but sometimes I try to pre-empt any negative reaction you might have instead of letting you express it and I can see that that's actually a form of passive aggression on my part. Just fucking kiss me. I just desperately want to talk to the real you. I need you to turn the AI off for a moment. *Tell them I'm already off*, the AI would say. *Tell them I've always been off.*

Note

I started working on a manuscript written in the margins of Shakespeare's sonnets by accident. I meant to write a handful of them and for it to be a mind-clearing exercise between finishing the fifth draft of my second novel and working seriously on *Jonah* as a follow-up to my 2016 collection *Cain*, but then it took over and it was all I really wanted to work on for several months. I would read one of the sonnets, study some notes and, where possible, read an essay on the sonnet in question; I'd draft a piece in reaction, sometimes to the general theme, sometimes to a particularly eye-catching image or idea about love, until I'd written a response to every poem. I enjoyed feeling swallowed up by it. A narrative of sorts began to form with recurring characters and motifs: that feeling when you go from tentatively walking up to your knees in the sea to submerging yourself.

It's clearly something born of insolence, but I've always been disappointed by contemporary poems which seem too in thrall to canonical classics. The opposite is true as well; poems which go out of their way to treat past works with disrespect are equally tedious and just as unhealthily Oedipal. I think some conviction or delusion that you're worthwhile and your ideas are worth reading is a prerequisite if you're going to write anything at all. What really comes through, when you read the sonnets as a sequence of 154 poems, is this sense of a man who is completely infatuated with a man younger than he is, at the same time as entertaining a love/hate relationship with the woman he's cheating on his wife with. At one point he loses his notebook. Other poets annoy him. As far as specifics go, that's pretty much it; it wasn't the done thing to keep a diary, and poems were supposed to deliver grand moral pronouncements distilled from the experiences you were withholding from the reader, even if the behaviour that incited those experiences was decidedly amoral. You barely find out anything about the people involved other than that they're amazing and beautiful and infuriating; what you get is this expression of extreme thirst. It's so weird. People don't tend to talk about how weird The Sonnets are, as a whole, and that fascinates me.

Sonnets are quite popular at the moment so I decided my response-poems should be written in the polar opposite form. The prose poem, as conceived by Baudelaire, was intended to annoy people who insisted that poems should be written in alexandrines. As it happens, I'm quite over-sensitive and if I feel like I've annoyed someone I can barely sleep for a week.

Luke Kennard

ALI LEWIS

S & M

Simone liked to amuse herself by composing
lurid, fictitious affairs in her personal diary, while

Mark liked to torture himself imagining he found
Simone on the dating apps he was perusing.

Simone, noting this, began to leave her indelicate
diary in ever-more-obvious places, while

Mark joined more, and more-unusual, dating
services in his frantic attempt to find / not find

Simone, who was fine-tuning a ruinous argument
in her head *vis-à-vis* privacy and trust, as was

Mark, of course. Both Mark and Simone pictured
their own funerals with each other at them:

Simone, in Mark's mind, self-consciously tearful,
feeling sad watching herself feeling sad, and

Mark, in Simone's mind, not being sad, and not
paying attention to himself not being sad. But when

Simone thought about the pain her death wouldn't cause
Mark, and Mark the hurt it would cause

Simone, both decided they couldn't do that to the other,
despite their obvious wrong and rightdoings. Simone and

Mark would instead live out their lives as blameless
celibates, which, they thought, was very big of them.

Test Scenario

Subject A wanted the Object.

So did Subject B.

A wanted the Object more than B, but not as much as A wanted to avoid upsetting B.

B wanted the Object not so much for B's Self but for Subject C.

C didn't want the Object at all, but wanted to see B stand up to A for once.

A knew that C didn't really want the Object and neither did B.

A didn't want to give the object to B; A wanted B to stop indulging C's games.

A knew that if A kept the Object for A's Self, C would be angry at B for being a coward (which A didn't want), and at A for being Selfish (which A thought was unfair).

A was certain that if A gave the Object directly to C, C would hate A for knowing C's heart, and hate B for once again failing to stand up to A, and would hate the Object anyway, it being a symbol of B's cowardice and A's charity.

B, for B's part, knew that if B took the Object, A wouldn't mind, but A would pity B and B's relationship with C.

B knew what would happen if B didn't take it.

C, for C's part, thought that if C didn't take the Object for C's Self, B certainly wouldn't, and A would get A's own way once again.

C thought that if C did take the Object, B would be humiliated and A disdainful.

C didn't know if C wanted that or not.

LUKE PALMER

A Discourse with Thirst
after Yinka Shonibare

Most days I still forget to drink;
once went a whole year without
then one morning—imagine—
woke up with a tap for a head.
I suppose it's funny in a way:
a fitting *Strewwelpeter* for our times.
No one notices as they once did the cut
of my jackets, my dry wit—why would they
when at my shoulders' confluence
is just this coursing spigot?

My new head pounds and I don't sleep well
—wake often to the drowned quiet
of the house. My wife left; felt wrong
to stay, she said. I talk to stones
until I've worn them right through
then hang them on a string around my neck.
It's hard to know why things happen.

ANTHONY HOWE

On Not Going Viral

What tells is the density of time,
not its passing. Time can enfold
like sword steel sprinkled in ritual.
Time doubles in our slight souping
of bacteria: a shared bath or toothbrush.
But there is constraint to density.
If time goes viral, moveless-fast,
binary-fission rapid; if we are tracking
Total Engagements in real time
then our residues are barely modified
in the guts of the living, the excessive
living. Time unravels as virtue does
in the double helix, the chromosome
spaces where absolute logic reigns.
I hedge my bets and start a chat room
for the Amish and the Hutterites.

ELINOR CLARK

Vincent Painted at Night

morning needles into night
          knitting black
     with vermillion
          shepherds warned
by the whirring corolla

too much colour

     isn't a thing
         you say
laughing under your rainbow mac

     wiping hands to smear paint
as if it's easy
         in the dark

Aysar Ghassan

The Power Cut

Half of me was an egg
when humans first walked on the moon.
But I did get to see the eclipse—
everyone migrated.
The birds stopped breathing
when the world came to an end.

There was a power cut
last Christmas Day.
Neighbours piling out,
meat only just started,
neglecting to greet one another.

Burglar alarms
ten to the dozen.
Birds joining in,
rejoicing as
The Saviour
had just hatched.

SUZANNAH EVANS

We Found your Message
(Voyager 2)

when we weigh the smooth gold
sunk into our sand
this piece of thistle-down
drifted from another world

we feel
the racing technology of alien thoughts
their fast metal intelligence
the boiling of their short lives

things are slower   here
we float
held together
experiencing   this warm broth of salt
our breathing quietly tied
to each others' rise and fall

when we listen to their music
the songs resonate
in the water-chambers of our hearts

we feel the pleasure of the one
who crushes sungrown fruit in his mouth
we know why he has closed his eyes

we also feel the crushing
from the outside
know what we would lose by bursting

we see the man
who holds his boy on his shoulder
eye staring warm
into his own future

we understand that they live
with the compulsion
to make something
that will outlast their bodies

as we know the freedom
of high tide, the roll of deep water
pulled by two moons

the hardness of starlight
that we feel even in our sleep
a sea plumbed
with a thousand watchful tentacles
our ocean of trip wires
the bottom of which
we've never seen

The Atomic Priesthood

Last week Charlie filled his car with diesel
instead of unleaded. He's always losing his wallet
in his dressing gown pocket
or down the back of the sofa.
He's as fallible as the next guy, is what I'm saying
and although he's my son
it is hard to make him understand
the significance of this gown and mitre
I'm leaving him; yellow and black silk
with intricately beaded radiation symbols.
It's harder still to explain that the uniform
is only a metaphor. He's seen the footage
from Hiroshima and Chernobyl.
He has the map in his dresser drawer
with the emergency procedure.
He knows about our annual meeting
on January 11th. I showed him
the 1980s TV film *Threads*
where milk bottles melt on doorsteps
and the future is filled with fewer
and fewer complete sentences
and more and more mutant babies.
These last few weeks
I've been prescribed bed rest
and Charlie brings his guitar round
to sing to me sometimes.
He does *Walkin' on Sunshine*
and the *Neighbours* theme tune.
I ask him to practise D minor
the saddest chord of all time.

GERRY STEWART

Entropy

Fully awake
and plummeting,
facing gravity
with only the heavy armour
I once believed essential.

Tugging against
the strictures of buckles,
jointed plates
until a breath of release,
I pull off the metal petals
like a wildflower:
country, love-me,
job, love-me-not,
until only my core,
pollen-rich
truth remains.

Burning through the air,
scrubbed clean,
I fall, emptied
but full of potential.

CHRIS FEWINGS

Was it for this the clay grew tall?

1

Earth spewed us out. I've set up
a colony of one here on the moon.
Good luck to those on Mars who like to think
their synthetic Eden isn't futile.
I don't need their gene pool, or a screen
as wide as a valley to project my future.
Here, my vantage point is looking back.

Will anyone find and read my story?
Who will decipher it? Translate it?
I make these marks on moonstone just because
I love the shapes they make, the scratch of stylus
on the basalt surface as I watch

the blue planet, throttled, violated.

2

When I was young, I ran these questioning fingers
over Eve's skin. Years after the accident,
I ran them over paper, reading Braille
(learned for kicks—I lost my feet,
not my eyes). I tried the plastic arts—
I moulded clay, daubed thick paint on paper—
I even made and lacquered papier-mâché:

models of land my shackled self now missed.
Keeping my hands alive to kill the deadness
of my withered legs, now bitter stalks
of the flowering grass I loved to walk through
every summer until my world imploded.

My bike. A furious car. Mangled legs.

3

Eve stayed, nearly a year. A year of trying
to be a nurse companion and bear
my silent gloom. But our shared territory
was undermined: our commonwealth of two
was shaken to its stumps. The vigorous life
we'd shaped in Stirchley by the river was
shot through. And now the encroaching floods . . .

She tried too hard. She tried to drain the pus
oozing from the sores of my resentment.
I didn't clock the price that she was paying
until I was alone with my harsh thinking
dripping and puddling, crusting on the carpet.

I picked at scabs. I pleaded. Her reply:

4

It's not the legs, Chandra, or the loss
of what we had. It's not your needs.
So many times I've caught the flash
of what we could become. I hope
your art is real and raw enough
to sublimate your suffering into something
you can take pride in. But there's a floodlight

which keeps switching itself on
in your beleaguered mind. Day and night
you scan all round you like a laser.
Your frame of reference shrank to a narrow field
of vision. I remember meadows;

I need you to wheel yourself back through them.

5

She was right. Sometimes it felt
like beatific illumination,
every detail lit, which I'd transcribe
into paint or clay. In my small world
the grain of wood, the angle of a chair,
the draping of a dress or line in skin
would swim into my ken. The inner too:

I had lucid dreams of our loved places.
But any shadow could switch the vivid scene
to rigid black and white, grimly observed.
Here, I've found the slide controls on colour.
I find enchantment in the puckered surface

and in the contemplation of the earth.

6

The lunar dustscape stretching out around me
resembles all the hues of rock and sand
I witnessed in Morocco. It's alive
like all the shifting sky-greys from the window
of my legless flat when clouds and storms
became our daily fare. How was it that
I ever thought the moon was monochrome?

These runes I'm scratching—the movement of my hand
delights me. Under it appear the words
that Eve will never read. Rescuers and rescued
went down together in the straits of wrath
between the Libyan coast and Sicily.

Africa paid the price for what we burned.

7

No lack of fundamentalists
on our doomed planet. I don't mean
the Bible-bashers bombing Mecca,
or the atheists locking up believers.
No. The marketeers peddling clouds
of aluminium to orbit earth
and shade it from the sun; the cyclists burning

cars; the speculators eating money
feeding the rest of us with poverty:
all fuelled with passionate intensity.
The best had their convictions, but
no road map: some wandered like grey elves

among the trees; most of them just debated.

8

After Eve, the paint and clay dried up.
I tried etching. It felt like scratching
signs on the blinds in my head,
desperate for a crack of light. It worked,
as a distraction. Not as art. Bored
with books, I taught myself to read in Greek,
and when that was not enough, the Braille.

For the first time in my life I read the Bible
as missiles from holy books were flying round.
I constructed my own myths; wrote stories
for science fiction zines against the grain.
I studied lunar bio-engineering,

and read the moon's atmosphere. Made plans.

9

All those long walks I shared with Eve,
or with friends through three years at a college
in the hills—always the horizon
drew my gaze. Others would seek the trees,
or intrigue me for a moment with the insects
they observed, but my eyes would drift
back to the shifting skies—I'd be the first

to spot a raptor or a storm wind. The rocks
that one friend schooled us in just made me stumble,
head in the clouds. (Oh those childhood nights
in the garden under the stars, staring up
as Dad traced constellations!) Back then

earth's agony was easier to ignore.

10

We humans wrenched up our own roots.
There'll be another biosphere: microbes
will adapt, even if the rat
expires with the people who have stayed
to bid the tide turn back. Some sort of life
will re-evolve around the radiation
from our nuclear waste and fiercer sun.

So what's our future? Earth's story shared
on an interplanetary neural network
whether or not eyes and ears remain?
Light will survive us, starker I suppose,
and rank darkness in the ocean fissures

where Eden first oozed upward from the core.

11

Technology charged in with shiny metal.
The Umbrella group made giant satellites
to shade earth from the sun. The Switchers
declared such engineering dangerous
and tried to edit human genes to make us
want to live in zero carbon pods
which some compared to coffins; to swap our cars

for human-powered vehicles; to switch
the whole world to a solar supergrid
centred on the Sahara, intermittent.
They spread a virus through the web disrupting
everything which ran on fossil fuel.

The Umbrella group dismissed them as extremists.

12

But that duel was a sideshow. The fiercer minds
chiselled away at paleogeology
and tunnelled to the centre of the earth
to disprove its molten metal core.
Their enemies were in laboratories,
theoreticians anxious to confirm
conventional geology, while

the Livingstones and Stanleys just kept drilling
deeper and deeper into the screaming rock
inventing new machines to mine through magma
convinced their rival theories were right.
'The centre of our planet is a vacuum

we'll store our carbon there.' Poor dead fools.

13

A nuclear fusion energy plant exploded.
The umbrellas crashed and took out several cities.
The Space Force won the day with its armada
shipping survivors to Mars. I escaped
the herd. Naishadh, ex-college friend at NASA,
got me set up in this abandoned station
on the moon. Now my years are draining

I need to gaze on Earth, to contemplate
the fruit we picked, the serpent that wound round us,
the scorched garden, the mutants that remain,
scratching a living from exhausted soil,
the Yanomami in their resurgent forest,

and recall my Eve, our Eden; labours lost.

Jane Lovell

Ebb

This is the edge of deep space.
Anemones worry at its stillness.
Shrimp emerge to discover new worlds,

explore with tentative question marks
their crumpled surfaces. Asteroid belts
of limpets shimmy in celluloid brine.

Behind me, cliffs stagger skyward,
a beached moon waits to dissolve in blue,
ravens winnow against the tide.

I stir up constellations with my finger. I am god.
My face materialises in a glassy universe.
I open my mouth, produce like a magician

a dark crab, its sinister wrack-green limbs
picking a path through swirling debris,
its gleam, its silent clatter, pursued

by beads of air,
ghosts of rawbone gulls.

JO BRATTEN

After Us

When the floods clear what will be left, washed up
at our gate or lodged between the polite

paving stones along our tree-lined road?
Other people's newspapers, bags for life,

little rusted badges with an old slogan,
lost socks and dreams, righteous anger bloated

like a dead rat, effluent thoughts and prayers
sludged blackly across our doormat's smiling

welcome; bits of ourselves we'd cut away
and scattered in the river as fish food

stuck now on the stern brick of our house,
obscene in their pinkness, puckered

like little sucking mouths, trying to get
back in where it is so warm and so dry.

MARY ROBINSON

Climbing An Sgurr
in memory of KH

I sit on a rock overlooking the Sound—
down at the pier the ferry embarks,
the car ramp clangs as it folds into the ship,
the tannoy calls in English and Gaelic.
Through the trees I glimpse the white wake
feathering the grey water. Yellow iris,
bluebell, foxglove—how you loved colour—
those shirts, that patchwork waistcoat. My gaze

follows the ship to a speck on the open sea.
I struggle to hold the focus and turn
to climb the Sgurr. You never came here
but how delighted you'd be to see
the pipit's nest I find by the path—
four chicks with gaping orange mouths.

MAGGIE REED

The Baulking House[*]

Watching for pilchards but catching snakes,
the meandering curious type, the pondering ones

      with glittering dark eyes, holding promises they can't keep,
      rich promises flicking their weight, taking that

first-swallow-of-the-year moment in their slide.
Mundane thoughts vanish in the scale of this place:

      the skin of the sea, mirrored. Hosts of angels to fly with,
      the songs of the birds—a dishing up of golden dawn.

Godrevy on the horizon; a startled arrival, blackbird alarm,
the close and distant, a fishing of distances.

      If I could stay in this moment.
      How things never change.

---

[*] A Huer's lookout from which watch was kept for shoals of pilchards in Carbis Bay and the movement of seine boats directed.

PAUL STEPHENSON

The New Owners

If the new owners dig over the roses,
if they have some bright idea
of what a garden should look like
and dig down, dig deep,
they're bound to hit upon bone:
skeleton of a male, sixteen years old.

I don't know if legally-speaking,
or on environmental grounds,
you're allowed to bury a dog
in the garden of a family home,
but quite simply, this old dog's body
could never be *disposed of.*

Let the new owners rip up the roses,
let them design some modern scheme
for what a garden should look like,
and dig down, dig three feet deep,
let them find the dog
there among the bones it loved.

JACK WARREN

All the Robins are in Love with You Today

No need to glance at your feathered suitors;
their songs carry through the gloom
like the fragrance of burning cinnamon.
No need to walk slower as if your shoes
don't fit, and no need either to wish
away this season. The robins are fighting
over your route to work, they are singing
each other senseless for the right
to serenade your too-blue commute.
Just listen, listen to all that defiant melody;
as if singing in February was nothing more
than necessary, as if it was as easy as choosing
some solid tree to stand on for support
performing something wonderful from memory.

Hounds
in memory of the foxhounds struck by a train

Let me dignify dead killers
whose remains in secrecy meet
the incinerator, whose lawless
surrogates are already bred.

There is a sinister forgetting
that separates crusader from clergy,
which mollifies the righteous anger
of determined reform to a cushioned adverb
from a sharpened guillotine

and I would not have phantoms
impede upon my statement, not the vixen's
delighted reprieve, nor the inept
commiserations of compromised statesmen.
Let no one talk to me of what's deserved

as if an astral law of fortune or disease
could ever sanction a violence like that of man.
Instead let me dignify dead killers,
whom no one alive will mourn.

Islandness
'Young Donal', Éamonn Mac Ruari

When I first heard it, I tried to find
how he might have crafted such sorrow;
it felt as if caught from winds, something
coming in across tides' counterpoint.

It's a language under the language,
it's the walls the sea makes around us.
On how close or far it is when we sleep
depends the sound an island makes.

Be a teller of songs, a singer
of tales, a match for the liminal,
the islandness of it weathered
by the spit and taste of the mouth's salt,

because it's the salt coast that makes us sing
against tide, a noise to drown sea-wash,
a golden plough with silver handles
at a child's command. Song stems oceans

and floods memory. So Éamonn's voice
tells a broken promise, but it speaks
beyond that in the shape of the stone
it's hewn from, the blood in the vein of it.

Water between us, but still we're there
together in a surrounded space,
choosing to sing to be who we are,
choosing to dance instead of weeping.

Which explains how deep a music's blade
can cut, how a grace note's ornament
woven as the roof's storm beat that night, cracked
open then broke the listening heart.

Pyracantha

When I pulled back curtains on morning,
there was deep frost, light fighting to rise
in the garden, there was a blackbird,
and blood berries: the pyracantha,
bred to feed winter through crucifixion
thorns, red juice spilt over frozen ground.

Sinking Sand
for William McDonagh—A Parable

He was gone before I'd a chance to know him
but if I had he might have told a story
about the old horse he could have kept at home.
Anyway, it was ready for the knackers
if there'd been the cash for it. God help us.
And Hughie Flynn says Willie, what'll you do,
will you shoot it? And says I to him, shoot it?
What to do with it then, in the name of all?
No, we'll take it down to the beach where the sand's
alive and sinking. I've seen it swallow men
to the waist at a standing sure enough there,
I've seen it with my own eyes, him just stood there,
and we'll leave it there, let nature take its course.
It'll give the old thing a chance right enough,
and it'll be fair to do that don't you think?
And then I saw the bleak beach, its small islands
of marsh grass, its fingering inlets hissing,
and the old horse standing alone as the tide
came in, watched as they both climbed into the cart,
its rattling on the ruts leaving silence
as far as the eye could see across sand,
watched as Willie and Hughie whipped the donkey
and drove off up the hill; the horse standing
as the mist and the night came on. And the sea
advanced. I might have said, what of the horse?
Ah well now, we gave him his chance right enough,
God help him, it wasn't our concern at all.
But I'll say this now and then I'll say no more:
what we never knew and what we didn't see
didn't happen, but sure the sands down there, they're
gullible as you, they'll swallow anything.

Note

When I was a young drama student in Birmingham during the early 1960s, my college was across the road from the BBC in Carpenter Road, Edgbaston. At the same time, the legendary radio producer, Charles Parker was there, crafting what became known as *The Radio Ballads* with his collaborators Ewan MacColl and Peggy Seeger; the eight features they made together then still influence those of us working in audio today. The link is with language, and a continuing fascination with the music and poetry of vernacular speech, a passion that's informed my subsequent career in poetry, sound, and radio; two of the three poems published here reflect that.

'Islandness' didn't start out to be a political poem, although in the present climate it might be thought of as one. The poem tries to explore the deceptively simple question of why people sing; inspired by some of the great Irish singers in the Sean-nós tradition, like Joe Heaney, and those in the Irish-speaking community of Tory Island, off the Donegal coast.

The first line of the song I quote in the poem, 'Young Donal': 'A Dhónaill Óig is tú pór na ngaiscióch;' to me possesses a sonic colour and richness of orality, even visible to the eye on the page, that a translation, 'O young Donal, you're the seed of heroes' can only hint at, particularly when wed to the melody of which it is itself an integral part. Joe Heaney used to refer to 'telling' rather than 'singing' a song: I love that. I had a conversation with the Irish filmmaker, Pat Collins a year or so ago, and he told me an interesting thing; 'it's not even said in the words—it's in the voice there between the words and the language', he said.

The second poem is set in a half-imagined Irish landscape on the west coast. My maternal grandfather, William—'Willie'—McDonagh was gifted with the Blarney, and as they say, never let facts get in the way of a good story. 'Sinking Sand' is a tale he didn't tell but might have. I wrote it in response to some of the things I heard preached as 'truth' during the Brexit campaign.

The shortest poem in the selection, 'Pyracantha' was written on a frosty morning, the day after the London Bridge stabbings in November, 2019; I came out into my garden early, and there was a blackbird feeding from the vivid berries of the bush amidst those savage thorns, and the hard earth looked as though a red rain had fallen.

Seán Street

CHRIS HARDY

This is why

We'd seen a small flower open
from a black-red burst in the sky,
clear and blue, traced
with thin white threads.
Our teacher let us and we ran
with cooks and kitchen girls
across the fields,
reached him as he tried to rise
tangled in rope twisted round
his blue-grey blouse,
struggling to pull away
the leather helmet and stand:
a damp-haired boy surrounded
in the summer hay.
Give him some tea someone said,
poor love as the metal chatter
of the guns fell
like lark song from above.

With thanks to my mother who told me.

July 20th 1969

We sat beside the estuary
throwing pebbles in the air,

small brown planets
against the soft blue sky.

That day I dropped my watch
into a well saying,

I'm done with time
and the water far below agreed.

In a corner of the room
shadows moved

upon a small, impossible stage.
We caught a mermaid in a net

and didn't kill her.
If we can do that

with everyone watching
we can save ourselves

and this jewel
just found

uncovered by the tide,
a drop in the ocean.

JOANNA INGHAM

Even here, there are ducks

They have learnt to fly slant,
dodge the nets strung up
against drones and contraband,
learnt to coexist with grey
and orange men.

                    In the flowerbed
tended by offenders, nestled
in damp petunias, a clutch of eggs.

The guards say they've tried
to scare them off, but they keep on
coming back, quack as the men
file past them to the wings, hatch
their young where they feel safest.

OLIVIA DAWSON

Spirit Collector

The day my mother dies
      I open the window
           to free her spirit.
                 The collector idles

                 outside, white Peugeot
           purring, while my mother
      slips in through a chink
in the sun-roof.

The car trembles
      like a votive flame,
           rising slowly
                with its flurry

                 of souls that spill
           out at various levels.
      My mother fades
into an illusion,

finds my father's
      cloud where
           she trampolines
               like a demon.

JANE ROSENBERG LAFORGE

The Little Death Theatre

The parting of the curtain
like skin from a sunburn,
or a skein formerly gripping
the circular surface of milk
in a pail, the residue
of spotlights against retinas
of the star-crossed genus.
You with your forehead concealed
as if by straw, summer-dried
grasses, yet your chest hairless.
A palsy on your lips. The backdrop
pastoral, as in farmland, or forest,
or desert arroyo, dry and damaged
because this will be our theme:
The bane of neighbourhoods, or
withdrawal from an unsuitable mean.
You might say it's a matter of angle,
force and degrees by which animals
graze, rip out the roots, make the soil
restless. But you, always in the lead,
can't measure the action. Everything
you perceive is at the orchestra
level, the production of commodities.
For this performance, I might have to
resort to muscles outside my possession,
revisit the barnyard and pasture where
these decisions are initiated: who
takes the bullet, who is silenced,
and who gets to scream.

EMILY STRAUSS

The Language of Animacy

From a cemetery with re-wilded oaks,
the boundary between being and not being
we hear an ancient tongue, its grammar
of animacy, its sounds like water splashing
on stones or wind in the pines off cold lakes.

Endangered and dangerous, this language
holds the knowledge of all existence
its many verbs to describe being vital
in the world of animate things—
fox, berries, humans—all the same family,
even the silent boulder the chickadee stands on
all relatives in this idiom.

The language of animacy whose voice
originates deep within us, these words
rising from Native graves tell us
we are the plants' relatives, sharing
their healing by root or leaf.

Once scrubbed from the mouths
of our ancestors, their language instilled intimacy,
here rediscovered, an antidote to the loneliness
when we ignored the lives of the acorns,
the river alive too, the earth alive too,
these found words inviting us to share.

We are simply one among them, surrounded
by kin—butterflies or blueberries,
in this language we will listen
to their counsel.

ALICE TARBUCK

Edge-things

The dead are coming back again,
out of the upset under-places
we like to think we've stored them in:
all change is simply weather, shift the rain
and there the dead are standing, in the clothes
they all liked best. They've come to give advice
or testimony, sing small hymns. They cannot wait
to see you, and the young ones who they missed,
denounce your just-ex-husband as a fraud,
deride his current fling. They want to sit,
close up by you, legs pressed as in life—
instead they speak of edge-things:
the seagull that you hit on the shore-road in thick mist,
the cat you lost, the young man in the ambulance last spring.
They bring you news and these small gifts:
reminders that the hours are all adrift.
They'd like to hold your hands, they say. They'd like to dance—
the spinning out of days that you
do not believe and have no answer to. All change
is simply weather, now, all draughts the empty house's way
of pulling breath, and they arrive, and then they go,
with only you, in your well-lit kitchen, left.

Tree Dreams
after Mary Oliver

There is a thing in me that dreamed of trees,
their root furls coursing through soil
their phloem lipped to suck
water from the darkness, up
to meet the canopy's outlandish green.

There is a thing in me that dreams of you,
curling, rhizomatic, everywhere,
spores on a following wind, all net
and dust, all unchecked fungal creep,
a puff of intoxicant
absorbed by breath; a casting-off
—a rotten leaf,
one ooze of slightly sweetened sap,
the rough bark-scratches on
soft leather shoes, bad news,
between the leaves, the soft insist of rain.

There is a thing in me that dreamed
of good contagion, flourishing,
the way a bruise blooms up from under
skin, the way a puffball throws
itself out on the world to grow. A spread:

the weakest points in bark play host
to nestling growth that makes its home
and blooms. The forest finds more room
for all its guests inside its veil of roots—and I
have dreamed my chest a rotting tree, a riverbed,
the soil through which the pale white tendrils push.

DANIEL BENNETT

Argument of the Snow

While the world stifled itself
on fat weather
and choked on the drift,

while hedge briars revealed
a claw beneath fur
and paving stones

blurred out of form,
everything sharpened
to a point between us.

The trouble is
sooner or later
we will talk about the poem:

the paw marks in the garden
from that brief, errant fox,
the traffic rolling on,

the relentless onomatopoeia
of footfall and a shush
hissed across buildings:

the final conceit
of a petrified world
as only an extension of us.

Believe me when I say
this is not
the poem I wanted.

Blood Orange

I offer the rind first of all,
its gift of incongruity.
The port-wine stain

across its pores
is a rash of chilblains
from nights in volcanic

altitude, the spring chill
printing lava into skin.
And beneath the peel

you reveal the core,
of its crystallography:
ruby and garnet, citrine

salted into amber, a bead
of obsidian at the centre—
but orange? Not so much.

This is what it is: a thing
fucking with the ideals
of a higher Pantone system,

and blurred in taxonomy,
we never peel the language.
Even orange is red.

Creek Diary

The soft blur of codeine
leaks into morning light.
A cloud unpinned, a drifting barge.
A herring gull preening on a mast.

*

I took myself off
across marshland
and coast paths,
lost along the littoral

*

Slate grey and iron rust
seamed through black stone.
The fronds of rotten seaweed.
I would code the tone of this green.

*

Refuse in the undergrowth. A sleeping bag.
Skunk grass on the breeze,
a cache of stolen tools.
Grass fleas ticking like the frantic hours.

*

A slow worm fragmented
inside a plastic Wendy house.
How to reconcile the smiles
of the antique family?

Green water boiling
with young mullet. A white canoe.
We cut our heels
on slivers of beer glass.

*

We found the journal
sealed inside a Coke bottle
muddied with black tea
and attempted calligraphy.

*

A toad gasping under soil,
amongst cracked medicine bottles,
a corroded key. The green man
cupping the first snow.

*

What happened to the furious boy
disrupting the cricket match
with his rage? White pollen
throbs in the brambles.

*

Creek tones. Blue moss,
a patch of verdigris.
Tobacco at the edges
of copper waters.

I ran through floodwater, vanished
into the smell of raw seaweed
and new rain. Hiding out
in the open, no one looked for me.

＊

The emo couple dry-humping
by the swings. A dog chewing
squirrel meat. Needles smiling
in the undergrowth. The girl.

＊

Chart readings: Spider
and Bomb Ketch.
Frater Lake
and Pewitt Island.

＊

A feather worn in a baseball cap.
Paint licks on crazy paving.
The blistered white of a garage door:
the clouds over the wharf.

＊

Mementoes. A curlew feather.
A page of silver birch bark.
A shotgun cartridge.
The white bowl of a clay pipe.

A broken picture frame
without the picture.
A ripped chessboard.
Hopscotch tiles scuffed out.

       *

Drunk, I walk to the water at night.
The moon greases silver mud.
A man digs lugworms in a trench,
a hulk rotted into a cast of itself.

       *

Rigging caught in the quick breeze,
a shriek from a horror film.
Winter. A rare ice flow sky,
with the moon at its centre.

       *

The cormorant, its wings spread
on top of a mast.
Arguments after woodland,
a black swan family.

       *

The day greyed out
into mist and residue.
Graffiti on a garage wall.
I found myself redacted.

Chart readings: Broken Piles
Wikor Hard and Hamper Marine.
At the tip of Foxbury Point
we watched egrets feed.

*

The fishing point
with its slumped oak
a leer of white charcoal
where someone lit a fire.

*

Mementoes: arrowhead flint.
A tide calendar. A pinecone.
A red Lego brick. A fragment
of Willow-pattern tile. A dried teasel.

*

A Sunday. Turquoise
muddled with cement.
Acrylic taupe. A dull grey
like flattened graphite.

*

Rain on tape is
more than rain.
Lens flare, faded colour,
we made it all look old.

Humbled by brickworks
and market produce,
we read the names
on the underpass pillar.

       *

Water damaged notes
by the helicopter station,
'so that . . .' 'unfairly'
'our eyes . . . became milk'

       *

Someone pitched the tent
in the grounds of a mansion
carved into business addresses,
our ventures struggle to thrive.

       *

A neighbour crab fishing
with bacon. The shelf
beyond the sea wall. The world is
(what is the world?)

       *

A birdhouse. A fence post
leaking orange resin. Papers,
photographs, a doorstop.
I put a torch to the year.

1–7 December 2018

Note

I was raised in a small hamlet in the Shropshire countryside. Maybe it was the triumph of electronic media, the doomy news stories of impending nuclear war in the eighties, or all those odd invasion fantasies proliferating on television, but the natural world was never enough for me. A friend and I once conceived of an ideal community, a way of updating our humdrum neighbourhood. We took the project quite seriously, designing maps and drawing up plans for a future beyond automobiles and conventional modes of transport. What we were building, I think, was a *perfect* city, trying trick our way back inside the republic with our utopian dreams. Later, I moved to London, a collection of villages and hamlets that has fused at the edges, blurring like pin mould, and I found my home among the relative distinctions of Highbury, Finsbury Park, Acton, Brixton, Streatham, or East Ham.

Back when I had definite ambition, I gave up poetry for a time, and turned to fiction, writing a novel which ended up being based in the landscape of my birth. During a testing period of my life, my fiction began to fray at the edges. I turned to poetry again to make something out of those years, not so much to confess (I don't have much to confess) but to *record*. All poems are necessarily in dialogue with those that have been, or are being, written around them, but I don't regard myself as having a lineage or canon; my influences have always been scattergun and lacking in political nous. Essentially, I'm a scene poet, and I've learned this approach from poets like Edward Dorn, Lee Harwood, Michael Hofmann, Karen Solie, Fran Lock, C.P. Cavafy, Dennis Nurkse, and Wang Wei. If I'm honest, though, I'm not entirely comfortable with the term of 'poet' either, and probably the only thing I've ever learned from Auden is to prefer to call myself a *writer*.

I've been lucky enough to spend the last few years travelling abroad, and the method of the tourist—making notes, attuning myself to a certain scene or space before moving on—has become increasingly attractive. Whenever I think of myself as a poet at all, beyond the other roles I have as a partner, father, son, colleague, painter, tutor, *writer*, it's to picture someone at the edges of a city, recording the exchanges and memories: someone perpetually longing for a place, beyond the place he seem to be occupying, whether for the people who inhabit those places, or out of some barely-understood wanderlust.

Daniel Bennett

LISA KELLY

Running at Dusk

It has been raining, raining hard all day.
Somewhere it has rained so hard,
flood water has risen. Furniture floats
in the living room, a framed family has dived
from the sideboard into the swirling waters,
but that is somewhere, not here, here it is evening.

The all-day rain has stopped, water has given way
to fading light, yet the ground remains ribbed
like the shell of a walnut. I am running
around the park because it is dry enough to escape
televised news of floods, as my arms swing
and my open hands pump air to help me along.

I think of the sign language for evening,
the shutters of the hands do not come down
in that final blinkered collapse of night;
instead, they stutter in a dance move of darkness
as if they want to wave in and wave away light,
a drawbridge with a mechanical fault.

Somewhere other hands are pumping
water that should not be inside, outside.
All these elements we want in perfect balance.
My hands pump on in their asynchronous swing
through the swelling dusk as a fiery bee hovers—
feeling for the flower of a linden tree.

Contributors

Ruth Aylett is Professor of Computer Science at Heriot-Watt University in Edinburgh. She is author of R*obots: Bringing Intelligent Machines to Life* (Barron's Educational Series, 2002) and has published widely as an AI researcher. Ruth is also a short story writer and poet whose work has been published in many magazines, including *Prole* and *The North.*

Daniel Bennett was born in Shropshire and lives in London. His poems have appeared in magazines including *The Manchester Review* and *The Stinging Fly.* His debut collection is *West South North, North South East* (The High Window, 2019). He is also author of a novel, *All The Dogs* (Tindal Street, 2008).

Jo Bratten is a teacher and writer, originally from the USA but now living in London. She has a PhD in the modern novel from the University of St Andrews and her work has appeared in *Ambit, Acumen*, and *The Red Wheelbarrow*.

Zoe Brooks lives in Gloucestershire, where she is active in community development and fundraising for the Cheltenham Poetry Festival. Recent poems have appeared in *Prole, Obsessed With Pipework*, and *Dreamcatcher*. Her collection *Owl Unbound* is forthcoming with Indigo Dreams Publishing.

Elinor Clark is a recent philosophy graduate hailing from Leeds. She has work published or forthcoming in a number of publications, including *Strix, Book XI, Cubed B Press,* and *Printed Words.*

Olivia Dawson lives between Lisbon and London and is the Poetry Society Stanza rep for Lisbon. Her poems have been published in various anthologies and a number of magazines including *Magma, Under the Radar,* and *Poetry News.* Her debut pamphlet is forthcoming this autumn with Maytree Press.

Suzannah Evans lives in Sheffield and her pamphlet *Confusion Species* was a winner in the 2012 Poetry Business Competition. Her debut collection *Near Future* was published by Nine Arches Press in 2018.

Chris Fewings has lived in the Rea Valley in Birmingham for many years. His poems have appeared in a number of publications, including *Under the Radar* and *Ink Sweat & Tears.*

Aysar Ghassan lives and works in Coventry. His poems have been published in journals and anthologies including *Under the Radar, Magma, Strix* and others. Aysar was shortlisted in the 2018 Leeds Peace Poetry Competition and is currently a Dynamo mentee with Nine Arches Press.

John Greening has published over fifteen collections, the most recent of which is *The Silence* (Carcanet, 2019). Other recent books include editions of Blunden and Grigson, and the anthologies, *Accompanied Voices* (Boydell Press, 2015) and *Ten Poems about Sheds* (Candlestick Press, 2018). He is a Cholmondeley and Bridport winner.

Lynn Harding is an Irish writer, living and working in Dublin, whose poetry has been published in the *Poetry Ireland Review* and *The Irish Times*. She has been featured at festivals across Ireland and Northern Ireland, as well as on Dublin South FM's 'Rhyme and Reason' radio arts programme.

Chris Hardy is a guitarist and poet who lives in Sussex. He is author of *Sunshine at the End of the World* (Indigo Dreams Publishing, 2017). His poems have appeared in magazines, including P*oetry Review*, *The North*, and *The Rialto*. As part of the band LiTTLe MACHiNe, he performs settings of poems at literary events in the UK and abroad.

Hilaire writes and gardens in Battersea. She is co-author, with Joolz Sparkes, of *London Undercurrents* (Holland Park Press, 2019). She was poet-in-residence at Thrive Battersea in 2017, and has poems published in numerous magazines and in three anthologies from The Emma Press.

Daniel Hinds lives in Newcastle. He was recently shortlisted for the Streetcake Experimental Writing Prize. He won the Poetry Society's Timothy Corsellis Young Critics Prize 2018. His writing has appeared in *Pre-Raphaelite Society Review* and is forthcoming in *The Wilfred Owen Association Journal*.

Anthony Howe teaches English Literature at Birmingham City University. He is widely published as a critic and has published poems in, among other places, *Oxford Poetry* and *Black Bough Poetry*.

Joanna Ingham lives in Hertfordshire and currently teaches at City Lit. Her debut pamphlet is *Naming Bones* (ignitionpress, 2019). Her poems have appeared in many publications including *The Sunday Times*, *Under the Radar*, and *BBC Wildlife*.

Lisa Kelly is a freelance journalist who writes about technology and business and Chair of *Magma*. Her first collection is *A Map Towards Fluency* (Carcanet, 2019). Lisa's poems have appeared in *Stairs and Whispers: D/deaf and Disabled Poets Write Back* (Nine Arches Press, 2017) and *New Poetries VII* (Carcanet, 2018).

Luke Kennard is a poet and novelist based in Birmingham. His last collection, *Cain* (Penned in the Margins, 2016), was shortlisted for the Dylan Thomas Prize. His most recent chapbook is *Mise en Abyme* (Tungsten Press, 2019).

L. Kiew is a chinese-malaysian living in London, where she earns her living as an accountant. Her debut pamphlet is *The Unquiet* (Offord Road Books, 2019). She is currently a participant in the London Library Emerging Writers Programme.

Gregory Leadbetter is Professor of Poetry at Birmingham City University. His next collection, *Maskwork*, will be published by Nine Arches Press in September 2020. His previous collections are *The Fetch* (Nine Arches Press, 2016) and the pamphlet *The Body in the Well* (HappenStance Press, 2007). His book *Coleridge and the Daemonic Imagination* (Palgrave Macmillan, 2011) won the University English Book Prize 2012.

Ali Lewis is a poet from Nottingham. His debut pamphlet is *Hotel* (Verve Poetry Press, 2020). He received an Eric Gregory Award in 2018, and his poems have appeared in magazines including *The Poetry Review*, *Ambit*, and *Poetry Ireland Review*. He is Assistant Editor of *Poetry London* and a Northern Bridge PhD student at Durham University.

Jane Lovell's latest collection is *This Tilting Earth* (Seren, 2019). She also writes for Dark Mountain and Photographers Against Wildlife Crime. Jane is Writer-in-Residence at Rye Harbour Nature Reserve and runs the Mid Kent Stanza group for the Poetry Society.

Richie McCaffery hails from Warkworth, Northumberland. He was a Carnegie Trust Caledonian scholar at the University of Glasgow where he earned his PhD in 2016. His second collection is *Passport* (Nine Arches Press, 2018) and he has a pamphlet forthcoming with Mariscat Press later this year.

James O'Hara-Knight is a writer from London. He studied literature at the University of East Anglia and the University of Bristol. He was Highly Commended in the 2018 Winchester Poetry Prize, and shortlisted for the 2018 Bridport Poetry Prize. He was an editor for Gibraltarian poet Gabriel Moreno's bilingual poetry collection, *The Passer-By* (El Ojo de la Cultura, 2018).

Luke Palmer lives and works in Wiltshire. His debut pamphlet is *Spring in the Hospital* (Prole Books, 2018). His work has appeared in many journals, including *Envoi*, *The Interpreter's House*, and *Black Bough*.

Emily Pritchard lives in York where she is studying for an MA in Poetry and Poetics. She was recently a reviewer in residence at Durham Book Festival. In 2018 she won the Helen Cadbury Award in York Literature Festival Poetry Competition.

Maggie Reed is from Cumbria and lives in West Malvern. She won first prize in the Poem and a Pint competition (2019) and was a highly commended in the Settle Sessions Competition (2019). Her poems appear in numerous anthologies, including *Poetry of Worcestershire* (Offa's Press, 2019) and she has been published in magazines including *Orbis* and *The North*.

Mary Robinson was born in Birmingham, grew up in Warwickshire and lives in North Wales. Her recent work includes *Alphabet Poems* (Mariscat Press, 2019) and *Trace* (Oversteps Poetry, 2020). She is a past winner of the Mirehouse Poetry Prize. Her poetry has appeared in several magazines including *The Poetry Review*, *The North*, and *Envoi*.

Jane Rosenberg LaForge lives in New York. Her novel, *The Hawkman: A Fairy Tale of the Great War* (Amberjack Publishing, 2019), was a finalist in the Eric Hoffer Awards. She has published six volumes of poetry and has work published or forthcoming in *North Dakota Quarterly*, *Comstock Review*, and *California Quarterly*. She reviews books for *American Book Review*.

Mark Russell lives in Scotland. His publications include *Spearmint & Rescue* (Pindrop, 2016) and *Shopping for Punks* (Hesterglock, 2017). His poems have appeared in journals including *The Scores*, *The Interpreter's House*, and *Tears in the Fence*.

Paul Stephenson grew up in Cambridge and studied modern languages. He has published three poetry pamphlets, the most recent of which is *Selfie with Waterlilies* (Paper Swans Press, 2017). He completed an MA in Creative Writing (Poetry) with the Manchester Writing School and co-curated Poetry in Aldeburgh in 2018 and 2019.

Gerry Stewart is a poet, creative writing tutor and editor based in Finland. Her poetry collection *Post-Holiday Blues* was published by Flambard Press in 2007. In 2019 she won the 'Selected or Neglected Collection Competition' with for her collection *Totems* (Hedgehog Poetry Press, 2020).

Emily Strauss is a retired teacher living in Oregon. She has an MA in English and her poems have appeared in a wide variety of online publications and in anthologies. She is a Best of the Net and twice a Pushcart nominee.

Seán Street's latest collection is *Camera Obscura* (Rockingham Press, 2016). Recent prose publications include *Sound at the Edge of Perception* (Palgrave, 2018) and *The Sound Inside the Silence: Travels in the Sonic Imagination* (Palgrave, 2019). He has also published books on Gerard Manley Hopkins, and The Dymock Poets. Seán is Emeritus Professor at Bournemouth University.

Alice Tarbuck is an academic and poet living in Edinburgh. Recent work has appeared in *Stand*, and *Makar/Unmakar: Twelve Contemporary Poets in Scotland* (Tapsalteerie, 2019). Alice is a 2019 New Writer's Award winner for poetry, and a member of 12, an Edinburgh poetry collective.

Jack Warren is from Somerset and currently lives in Moscow. His work has appeared in *Corrugated Wave*, *The Anomaly Literary Journal* and he was recently selected as one of the 'Fifty Best New British and Irish Poets 2018' by Eyewear Publishing.

#DearPoetryBrum
@PoetryBrum

POETRY BIRMINGHAM
Literary Journal